I am an Arabian Oryx

Aaron Carr

www.av2books.com

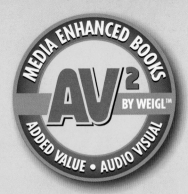

MEDIA ENHANCED BOOKS

AV² BY WEIGL™

ADDED VALUE • AUDIO VISUAL

Go to www.av2books.com, and enter this book's unique code.

BOOK CODE

D 1 3 1 4 5 3

AV² by Weigl brings you media enhanced books that support active learning.

AV² provides enriched content that supplements and complements this book. Weigl's AV² books strive to create inspired learning and engage young minds in a total learning experience.

Your AV² Media Enhanced books come alive with...

Audio
Listen to sections of the book read aloud.

Video
Watch informative video clips.

Embedded Weblinks
Gain additional information for research.

Try This!
Complete activities and hands-on experiments.

Key Words
Study vocabulary, and complete a matching word activity.

Quizzes
Test your knowledge.

Slide Show
View images and captions, and prepare a presentation.

... and much, much more!

Published by AV² by Weigl
350 5th Avenue, 59th Floor New York, NY 10118
Website: www.av2books.com   www.weigl.com

Library of Congress Cataloging-in-Publication Data
Carr, Aaron.
 Arabian oryx / Aaron Carr.
   pages cm. -- (I am)
Audience: Grades K to 3.
 ISBN 978-1-62127-280-9 (hardcover : alk. paper) -- ISBN 978-1-62127-286-1 (softcover : alk. paper)
1. Arabian oryx--Juvenile literature. I. Title.
QL737.U53C276 2014
 599.64'5--dc23

                    2012046231

Printed in the United States of America in North Mankato, Minnesota
1 2 3 4 5 6 7 8 9 0 17 16 15 14 13

032013
WEP300113

Senior Editor: Aaron Carr   Art Director: Terry Paulhus

Weigl acknowledges Getty Images as the primary image supplier for this title.

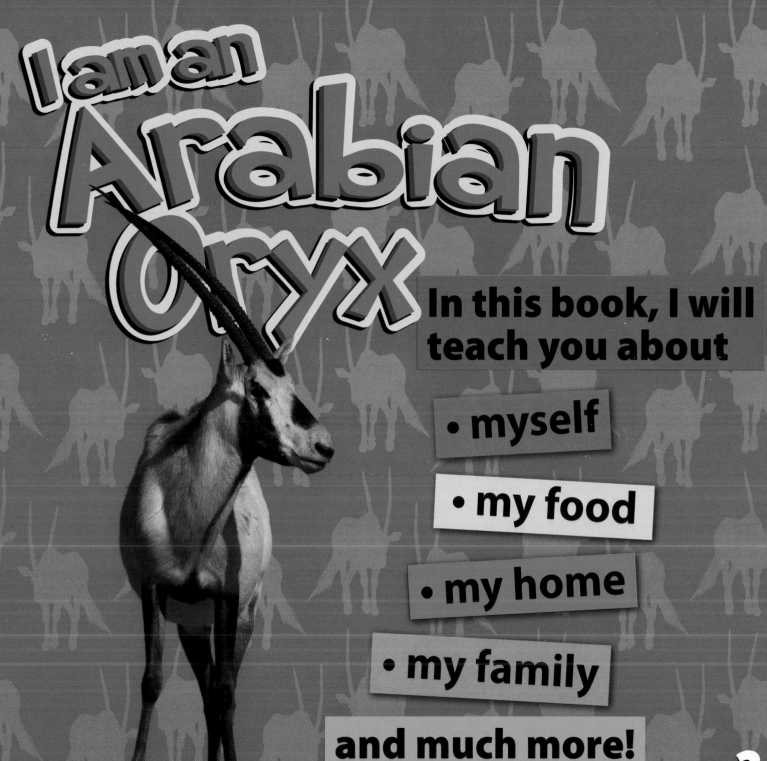

I am an Arabian Oryx

In this book, I will teach you about

- myself
- my food
- my home
- my family

and much more!

I am an Arabian oryx.

5

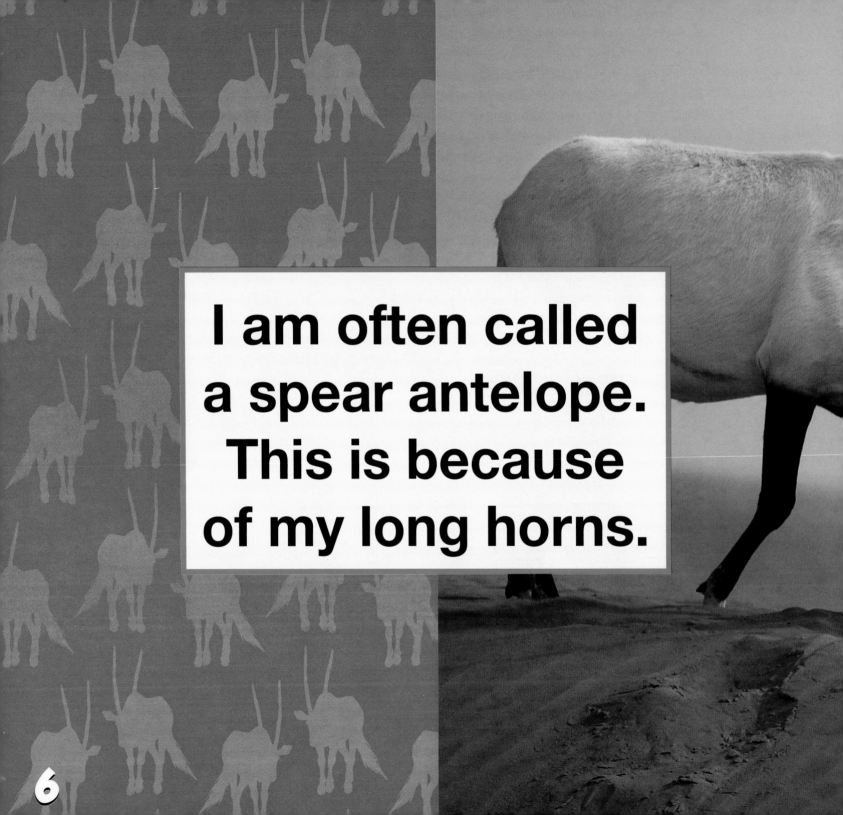

I am often called a spear antelope. This is because of my long horns.

I have wide feet.
They help me walk
in the sand.

8

I could walk and run one hour after I was born.

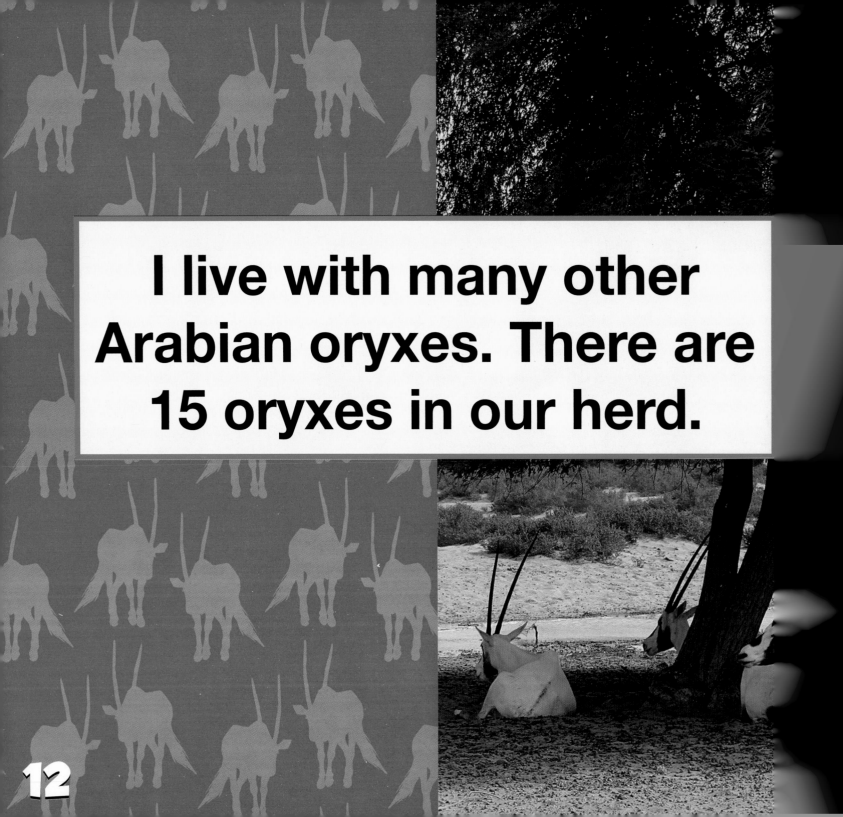

I live with many other Arabian oryxes. There are 15 oryxes in our herd.

13

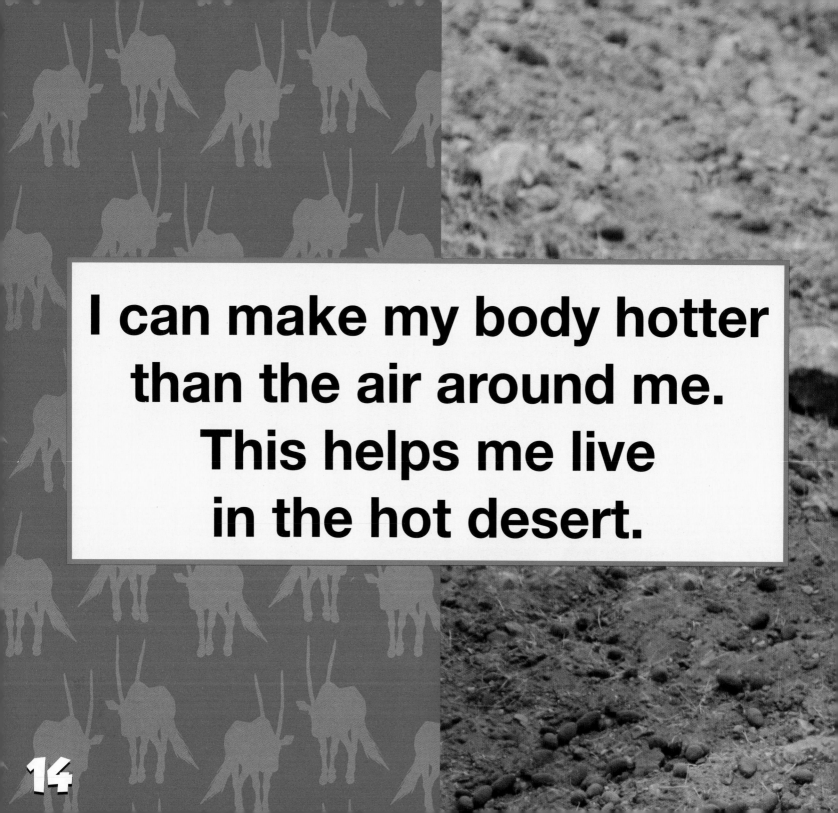

I can make my body hotter than the air around me. This helps me live in the hot desert.

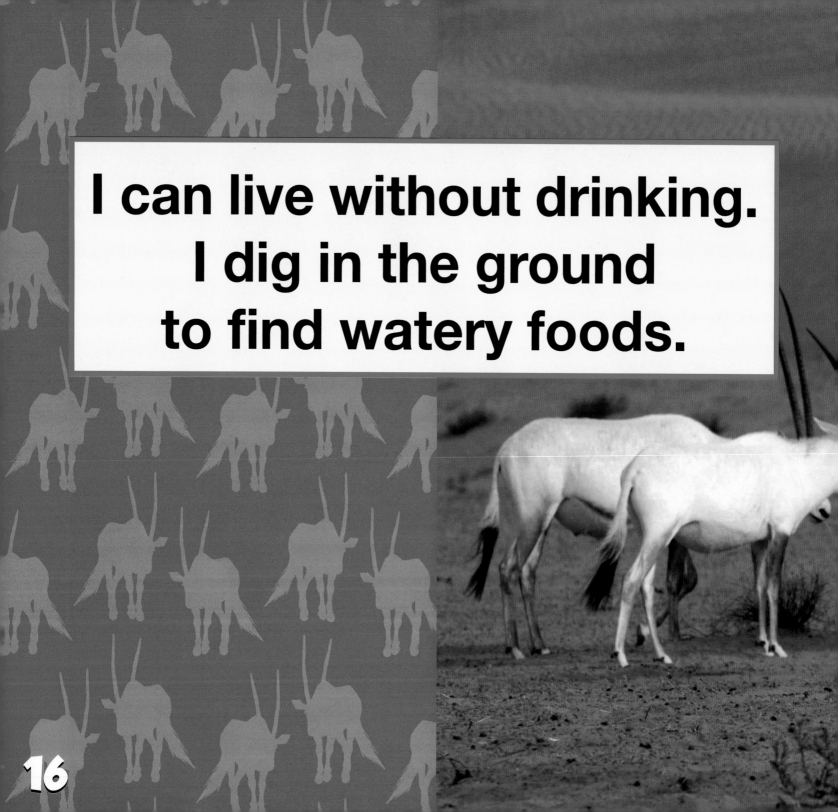

I can live without drinking.
I dig in the ground
to find watery foods.

I can tell if it is raining in places very far away.

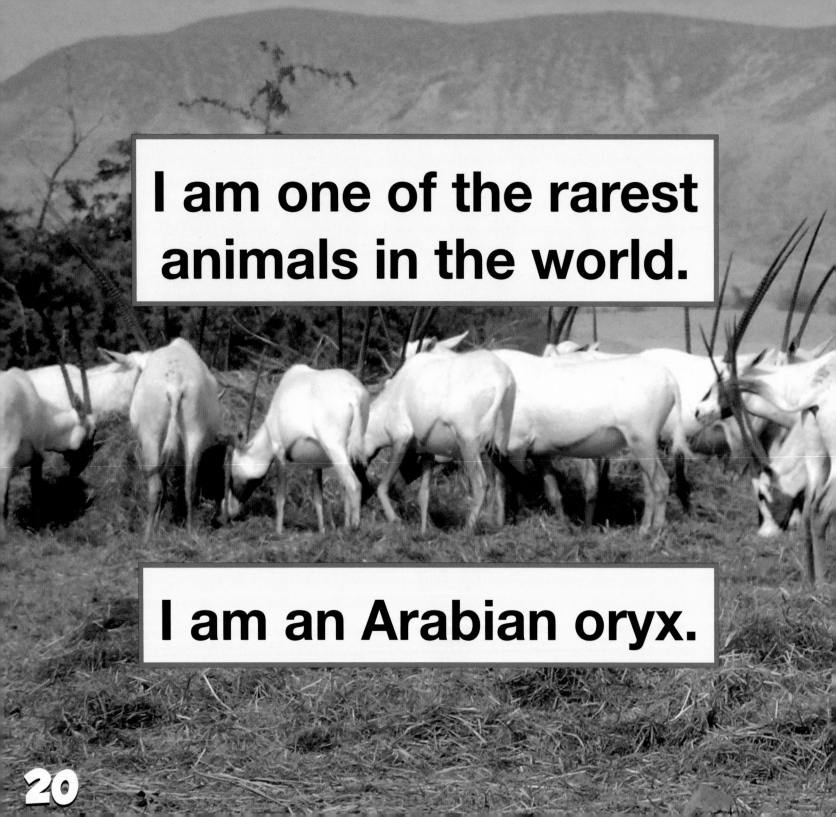

I am one of the rarest animals in the world.

I am an Arabian oryx.

ARABIAN ORYX FACTS

These pages provide detailed information that expands on the interesting facts found in the book. They are intended to be used by adults as a learning support to help young readers round out their knowledge of each amazing animal featured in the *I Am* series.

Pages 4–5

I am an Arabian oryx. The oryx is a type of antelope. It is related to cattle, sheep, and goats. There are three species of oryx. An adult Arabian oryx is 3 to 4 feet (0.9 to 1.2 meters) tall and weighs up to 165 pounds (175 kilograms).

Pages 6–7

I am often called a spear antelope. The Arabian oryx is best-known for its two long, straight horns. These horns can be up to 58 inches (147 centimeters) long. Male and female oryxes have horns. They use their horns to protect themselves from other animals.

Pages 8–9

I have wide feet. They help me walk in the sand. The Arabian oryx has long, thin legs and wide hoofs. The hoofs are splayed to help the oryx to walk and run in deep sand. The Arabian oryx lives in the sandy deserts of the Arabian Peninsula in the Middle East.

Pages 10–11

I could walk and run one hour after I was born. Oryx calves must be able to follow the herd, which is always moving. A calf will drink its mother's milk for the first four months of life. An oryx is full grown after about two years.

Pages 12–13

I live with many other Arabian oryxes. There are usually about 10 to 15 oryxes in a herd. Herds of more than 100 have been spotted in nature. Oryx move constantly, seeking food and water. Females, or cows, lead the search. Males, or bulls, stay behind to protect the rest of the herd from predators.

Pages 14–15

I can make my body hotter than the air around me. The Arabian oryx can raise its body temperate up to 116° Fahrenheit (47° Celsius). It then gives off heat to the cooler air around it. This helps the oryx maintain a safe temperature without losing moisture by sweating.

Pages 16–17

I can live without drinking. The Arabian oryx can live for weeks without water. During this time, it will get the water it needs from the plants it eats. Oryxes will dig in the ground to find water-storing plants, such as roots and tubers.

Pages 18–19

I can tell if it is raining in places very far away. Oryx herds have been known to walk more than 50 miles (80 kilometers) to track recent rainfall. They like to feed on the grasses and other types of vegetation that sprout after rain.

Pages 20–21

I am one of the rarest animals in the world. By 1972, hunting had almost wiped out the Arabian oryx. There were only six left in the world. A few of these were sent to zoos for breeding. Today, there are more than 1,000 Arabian oryxes in nature, with another 6,000 to 7,000 in captivity.

KEY WORDS

Research has shown that as much as 65 percent of all written material published in English is made up of 300 words. These 300 words cannot be taught using pictures or learned by sounding them out. They must be recognized by sight. This book contains 48 common sight words to help young readers improve their reading fluency and comprehension. This book also teaches young readers several important content words, such as proper nouns. These words are paired with pictures to aid in learning and improve understanding.

Page	Sight Words First Appearance
4	am, an, I
6	a, because, is, long, my, of, often, this
8	feet, have, help, in, me, the, they, walk
10	after, and, could, one, run, was
12	are, live, many, other, our, there, with
14	air, around, can, make, than
16	find, foods, to, watery
18	away, far, if, it, places, tell, very
20	animals, world

Page	Content Words First Appearance
4	Arabian oryx
6	antelope, horns, spear
8	sand
10	born, hour
12	herd
14	body, desert
16	ground

Check out av2books.com for activities, videos, audio clips, and more!

1 Go to av2books.com

2 Enter book code D 1 3 1 4 5 3

3 Explore your oryx book!

www.av2books.com